Book 2 of the Decency Journey series

HEALTHY ORGANISATIONS

Anna Eliatamby

ISBN: 978-1-80443-009-5

British Library Cataloguing in Publication Data.
A catalogue record for this book is available from the British Library.

This pocketbook also contains some concepts from
the 2022 book *Healthy Leadership and Organisations:
Beyond the Shadow Side*. Anna Eliatamby, Editor

PREFACE

This pocketbook is part of a series on healthy leadership and organisations for decency. The aim is to encourage you to look at what is golden and shadow in your work as leaders and as organisations, so people can detox and heal. When we focus on the golden, and address the shadow, then we are more likely to be decent in all we say and do.

Decency is 'honest, polite behaviour that follows accepted moral standards and shows respect for others' (Oxford Learners Dictionary).

We all contribute to what is golden (positive) and shadow (negative) in work and life. Mostly we operate from the golden side, but sometimes we function from the shadow side, and this holds us back as individuals and as organisations. We are all human and fallible.

Let's give ourselves permission to explore the positive and negative so that we create a better balance between the golden and shadow for ourselves and the wider world community. This way, we can contribute to a healthier world both for us now and for the generations to come. And we may yet achieve better decency for us all.

The titles in the Decency Journey Series are:

Healthy Leadership
Healthy Organisations
Coping In A Toxic Environment
Your Own Toxic Work Behaviours
Building an Organisational Mental Health and Well-being Strategy
Volcanoes, Personal Healing and Change
Our Journey for Diversity and Inclusion in Business

CONTENTS

INTRODUCTION

Hello and welcome. How many organisations have you worked in that contained at least a little toxicity? And how many research reports do you know of that highlight the presence of toxicity in organisations? Too many.

There are several interventions that are used to help to change organisations and leadership so that they can become more golden, respectful, and decent. Their overall focus is to improve business and leaders. So why do toxic elements still persist?

Is it because we promote the positive, but are reluctant to face the risk of naming and tackling the negative and awful? If we avoid facing the negative, then we are deliberately allowing staff to work in unhealthy environments that severely affect their well-being and lives. Productivity is adversely impacted, and we permit a culture of impunity for those who continually function from the shadow side.

We must do both, as recommended by the UK Financial Reporting Council and the UK Chartered Institute of Internal

Auditors. Addressing toxicity and enhancing the positive very clearly leads to an organisation with a healthy culture in which people are collegial, and leadership is respected, trusted, and supportive. People stay and want to work in these businesses.

Let's remember our courage and take the risk of tackling the negative <u>and</u> promoting the positive. It is necessary for us, those affected, and the legacy we want to leave.

Here is a model with some questions and exercises for you.

DEFINITIONS

WHAT IS OVERALL HEALTHINESS?

The words 'healthy' and 'healthiness' refer to physical health and, sometimes, mental health and well-being. All these facets are important components for overall healthiness, but we suggest that there are others. These include synergy between purpose, values, and how we live and work; the impact of material resources and the environment, being willing to be open and listen to the incoming future, and how we live and cope with the shadow side. All these factors, for overall healthiness, need to be coordinated with compassion and respect by our individual or organisational sense of Self. Collective responsibility for promoting the positive and addressing the negative should be present.

The golden refers to the positive parts of us (kindness, integrity) and of organisations (compassion, working with purpose). The shadow includes dishonesty, bullying, and harassment for individuals and organisations.

Healthiness is an essential ingredient for decency. Without it, we are likely to be unsuccessful.

WHAT IS HEALTHY LEADERSHIP?

Leadership is an individual and collective function that has many intentions. This usually includes an aim to serve human beings and/or something else. Some people operationalize leadership ethically and positively to serve others. Others will have another focus, such as a profit motive, alongside wanting to be ethical.

Healthy leadership happens when the individual or the group do their utmost to serve others ethically and respectfully, while acknowledging that there can be negativity and being willing to address it and heal. They remain flexible and open to sensing the incoming future.

Being and growing as a healthy leader ensures decency in yourself and in how you act at work.

WHAT IS A HEALTHY ORGANISATION?

Why do organisations exist? To enact a greater purpose, sometimes forgotten as the organisation becomes bigger and veers from the intended path.

A healthy organisation ensures it remains true to its purpose, and does no harm to humans or the planet. <u>Do no harm</u>. The organisation always endeavours to provide a nourishing culture and structure within which people can grow and flourish in their work to achieve that purpose. A healthy organisation works to recognise and address unhealthy elements, is amenable to change, and will consider possible futures while operating in the present.

Decency is seen as a core essential and its use flows naturally throughout the organization. People do not have to think about the need to be decent, they just are. Thus, the organization contributes to the greater decency we need for the world.

OUR MODEL

ORGANISATIONAL

Wider world

Being and doing
(individual and group)

Community

Legislation, policies
and procedures,
organisational structures

Coordination
for overall
health

Well-being, mental health
and physical health

Values, ethics and purpose

Physical and material
resources and the
environment.
Where people work

Diversity, equity, and
inclusion

Organisational
Self

Formal and informal
leaders

Culture and work
practices

Emotions, cognitions,
physical and relationships

Organisational history (known and unknown)

The diagram contains only dotted lines on purpose, as every aspect is porous and interconnects with all the other facets that are shown. All the components contribute to the overall healthiness of the organisation beyond well-being, mental health, and physical health. All elements contribute to the Organisational Self, which then guides the collective in terms of behaviours, thoughts and feelings, and interactions with each other.

The wider world and community affect employees and the organisation. For example, consider how the need for sustainability impacts all parts of a business.

How the administrative structure works has an influence on behaviour and culture.

Values, ethics, and purpose—how they exist and are implemented (or not) have an effect.

Formal and informal leadership can make or break employees and culture.

Individual and collective well-being, mental health, and physical health shape how employees' function.

We link well-being, mental health and physical health to emotions, cognitions, physical (body), and relationships; all these are affected by every other factor in the diagram.

Material resources and the environment where people work is influential.

We construct the Organisational Self from the culture, behaviours, and the golden and shadow aspects which underpin all other aspects. These influence people and their work.

The organisational history is the stage upon which the other aspects operate.

We use this model throughout the pocketbook.

THE INITIAL ASSESSMENT

Every organisation has a culture with positive and negative aspects, some of which are articulated and others not. The accepted behaviours of most employees, including leaders, contain a mix of golden and shadow behaviours depending on what is acceptable in the current zeitgeist. The golden and shadow impact every aspect of the organisation.

In the table below are some examples of golden and shadow elements.

Golden	Shadow
Self-esteem, compassion, kindness, optimism, respect, decency, honesty, transparency, humility, well-being, integrity, diversity, equity, and inclusion, communication, building relationships, collaboration, happiness, courage	Arrogance, manipulation, cruelty, insincerity, stubbornness, sneakiness, misusing banter deliberately, compassion fade/fatigue, hypocrisy, lying, dishonesty, laziness, malicious gossip, prejudice, discrimination, hubris, jealousy, envy, pessimism, competitiveness, revenge, psychopathy, sociopathy, Machiavellianism, narcissism, self-sabotage, underperformance, bullying, harassment, fraud, corruption, willful blindness, agnotology, suppression, plagiarism, fear, anger

There are three approaches to having a positive and inclusive perspective or veering towards negativity.

1. Be inclusive and work for fairness, respect, and decency. Willingly address any negativity that arises and promote the positive. Expect collective accountability from all for both golden and shadow behaviours.

2. A second group may work for inclusion, but also benignly neglect any toxicity that is present. Sometimes this inattention occurs unconsciously through denial and ignorance, so the awful culture of the organisation continues, perhaps for years, even if people leave because of it.

3. The third group, especially in very toxic environments, will malignantly contribute to, or ignore, the noxiousness.

It is important to identify the quantity and quality of toxicity that is prevalent if you want to explore the golden and shadow elements present in your organisation. It will determine how you carry out the investigation.

Where would you locate your organisation on this scale?

<-->

Inclusive   Benign neglect of the positive   Malignant neglect of the positive

Who are the key groups, cliques, and individuals?

How powerful are they?

Where would you locate them on the continuum?

Which individuals and groups could help you?

Who could block or sabotage your efforts, either actively or through simple inaction?

Who may need to leave?

The readiness to explore will depend on how you have assessed your organisation in terms of the presence or absence of inclusiveness. If you are an inclusive organisation, then there is likely to be a readiness to investigate, with representation from all parts of the business.

If there has been some benign neglect, even in one section, then it may be difficult to have an open investigation. You may need to start with a process of trust building and stating that the organisation, while having positive aspects, must also consider the negative in an honourable and non-punitive manner. Demonstrate your intention with action, perhaps by declaring how you have been complicit. You may need to start with anonymous reporting and then move on to more open processes.

If there has been malignant neglect, then it is customary for an investigation to be mandated. Some may be relieved that the issues are being investigated, but many could be obstructive. The intention of the investigation needs to be made clear, including that all need to take part honourably. Again, it is worth modeling what you expect others to do.

Identify the key issues that the organisation wants to prioritise and address. A comprehensive assessment could be the issue.

1.

2.

3.

Please consider the questions below for each of the prioritised issues.

How is the issue affecting the organisation?

What are the origins of the issue?

What is the balance between the golden and shadow parts? Which is more preferred and how is it maintained?

How much does being decent matter?

What promotes well-being, mental health, and physical health?

How is the issue affecting the ability of the organisation to achieve its purpose and mission?

To what extent is the organisation's history having an effect?

How facilitative is the organisational culture and leadership (formal and informal)?

To what extent is the Organisational Self known, recognised, and influential? To what extent does the Self coordinate what happens? How is the overall health of individuals and groups in the organisation? How open are they to the future?

Please summarise your findings here, and then answer the questions that follow.

If people select change, then how easy or difficult will it be to adjust?

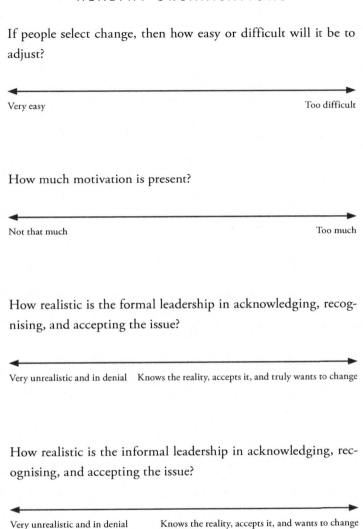

Very easy   Too difficult

How much motivation is present?

Not that much   Too much

How realistic is the formal leadership in acknowledging, recognising, and accepting the issue?

Very unrealistic and in denial   Knows the reality, accepts it, and truly wants to change

How realistic is the informal leadership in acknowledging, recognising, and accepting the issue?

Very unrealistic and in denial   Knows the reality, accepts it, and wants to change

How willing is the leadership (formal and informal) to take risks?

Not at all — Willing — Too willing

What is the balance between the golden and shadow parts of the leadership and organisation?

Very unbalanced — Absolute harmony

How realistic are the staff and other stakeholders in acknowledging, recognising, and accepting the issues?

Very unrealistic and in denial — Know the reality, accept it, and want to change

How much courage for change is present?

Very little — Too much

How willing are people to take risks?

Not a lot — Too enthusiastic

How much energy for this change is available?

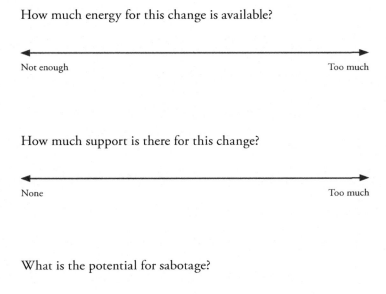

Not enough   Too much

How much support is there for this change?

None   Too much

What is the potential for sabotage?

None   A massive amount

Consider your answers and reflect on whether this is the right time. Sometimes it is best to wait.

> *Toni (pronouns-they, them), on starting their job as the deputy CEO, knew straight away that this was, as rumoured, a very toxic place. The board had brought them in to clean it up, knowing that this was an impossible task. Toni waited until they had a broader understanding of the situation and had a cohort of support within the board and leadership.*

If it is not the time to bring about large-scale change, then what can you do to make the situation more positive for the staff?

While waiting, Toni quietly and surely encouraged the managers to build in more care and support for the targeted staff. A few perpetrators were spoken to and encouraged to change.

Our decision is…

That public report highlighted so many awful issues that we knew about but did not address. The board and leadership must tackle this. We have agreed upon a plan, starting with a public meeting. There was no reaction to our statement that things needed to change. We are going to press ahead regardless. I wonder who will work with us and who will sabotage us.

꿍꿍

Thank goodness, we are finally tackling the toxicity in the department. We are all relieved that we don't need to suffer in silence anymore.

THE DEEPER ASSESSMENT

Please ensure that you are as inclusive as possible when carrying out this assessment. This will increase the likelihood of your plans for change succeeding because other people have taken part. Looking at both the positive and the negative is essential.

There are many methods for assessing the psychological health of an organisation. It is best to create a small group who represents the organisation, from the very senior to the most junior, to choose and carry out the assessment.

Include **quantitative data**, such as:

  sick leave
  number of performance-managed staff
  number of complaints about bullying and harassment
  usage of internal justice systems
  surveys on staff views
  well-being and mental health interventions

The British Standards Institute and MIND (UK mental health charity) have assessment processes to look at well-being (physical and mental health); others look at occupational health and safety. While none of their processes directly compare golden and shadow aspects, they can provide valuable data. Some could adopt a more **qualitative** approach (such as a large-scale event at which sufficient representatives from the different layers of the organisation come together to look at a model (such as the one described above) and provide their views and reflections so that they can develop a perspective from which to act. A range of focus groups could also be used.

You could identify key qualities that encourage people to look for the change you want to introduce. It will remind them of what is already in place, both positive and negative.

Perhaps you could use a pulse survey that contains areas both highlighted above and outlined below. They are used to find out how staff feel about given issues and can be done frequently. Topics for the survey could include:

trust in leaders and managers
ease of communication with them
whether staff feel able to discuss errors
motivation and courage
the presence or absence of professional behaviours
impact of negative actions
whether the culture is conducive and positive
level of inclusion present
whether systems such as communication, HR, and internal justice are functional.

It is best to choose 8–10 items for the survey.

We recommend you pick a method that is inclusive and reflective of your purpose for the change. For example, if you want to encourage openness, then the assessment process must reflect that.

Two very helpful and inclusive methods are "Building Community Resilience" and "Asset Based Community Development" (John McKnight). We can adapt both for organisations. These can start with the community of concern defining its vision, then creating questions and processes to investigate the current situation against the vision, followed by a community map of assets and areas for growth and then a plan for change, based on the map.

KEY QUESTIONS TO CONSIDER

Regardless of the methodology you choose, here are some questions to think about. Please choose the most important ones.

What are the issues/behaviours of concern that need to be addressed?

How much do you know about the organisation's history?

What have you assumed about the growth of the organisation?

How has the past influenced the present?

What words would you use to describe the organisational culture and work practices? Who keeps it alive? What groups and cliques exist (formal and informal) to maintain the culture?

To what extent is there alignment between the organisation's purpose and the promotion of well-being, mental health, and physical health?

What are the organisation's stated values, ethics, and purpose? How much do they steer the behaviours in the organisation? How much does the purpose fit the world of today? Who believes and enacts the values, ethics, and purpose? Who does not and why?

What is the quality of the physical environment and abundance of material goods, including salary?

Who supports inclusion and prevents discrimination? Who does not? What do the different groups and individuals do to promote or subvert inclusion?

How inclusive is the organisation? How much do diversity, equity, and inclusion matter?

What is the overall approach to courage and risk-taking? How positive is it? From where was it learned and what maintains it? What more could be done?

What levels of hope and motivation are present? Who encourages them? Who does not? What else is required?

How important are compassion, respect, and decency? How are they shown?

How well does the physical environment promote and facilitate golden behaviour as opposed to shadow actions?

In terms of legislation, policies, processes, and organisational structures, how much do they reflect and promote the golden positive side, e.g., the use of compassion; and how much do they focus on the shadow and negative?

(For example, most human resources policies concentrate on actions to take if there are aberrant behaviours. Of course, some do also describe codes of conduct, but it is often assumed that staff will behave accordingly. And there is usually very little about how to promote and support compassion and decency in staff, either of their own volition or through management and leadership practice. We have yet to see a procedure that describes the need to be respectful, kind, honest, compassionate, and inclusive in such a way that employees understand what to do differently.)

How responsible is the organisation to the wider world and community? What is the influence of the wider world and community on the organisation and vice versa? How important is the global need for sustainability? What do people do to facilitate sustainability?

What is the accepted list of golden and shadow behaviours and associated work practices? How are they activated? Who promotes them, and who blocks or tries to stop them? Describe their function—helping, or preventing the golden?

Who are the formal leaders and informal leaders? Who has the most power and influence? To what extent is each group working on the golden and/or shadow side?

What is the quality of relationships that are present, both formal and informal? How supportive are they? Who are the cliques?

How much support is there for learning and development?

Locate everyone (both individuals and groups) you know on this graph. It will help you identify who is golden and who is shadow.

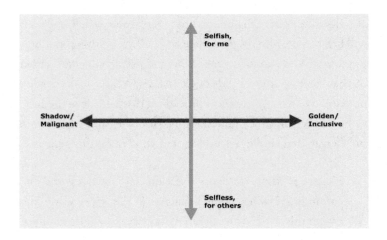

Which emotions are permissible? Which ones are not?

What are the prevalent styles of thinking and decision-making? How helpful are they?

How would you describe the collective Organisational Self?

Who, or what department, keeps coordinates and maintains it? For example, is there an informal dress code and/or an informal list of behaviours that are acceptable or unacceptable?

How flexible are the staff in the organisation? How open are they to the new and unexpected?

Describe the overall health (mental and physical) of the staff. Identify the factors which impede overall health and those which facilitate it.

Outline the connection between the Organisational Self and the golden and shadow.

WHAT HAVE YOU LEARNED?

You could use this table as a guide to write your key findings.

Area	Description
Sense of Organisational Self and coordination	
Compassion, respect, and decency	
Well-being, mental health, and physical health	

Emotions, cognitions, physical (body), and relationships	
Hope, courage, risk-taking, and motivation	
Organisational history	
Presence and use of golden and shadow behaviours	
Values, ethics, and purpose	
Interacting with the wider world and community	
Material resources and environment	
Where people live and work	
Diversity, equity, and inclusion	
Administrative issues	

Formal and informal leadership and relationships	
Anything else	

Based on the above, what have you learned about the Organisational Self and its coordination, openness to the future, and role in overall health and associated leadership?

Organisational Self	

Therefore, what type of organisation are you? Where would you locate yourself on the continuum between golden and shadow using the health levels described below?

OVERALL HEALTH LEVELS

Now that you have carried out your assessment, what rating would you give the organisation?

Platinum—an abundance of golden behaviours in many aspects of an individual or organisation; the golden is present and available 95% of the time or more. You address any minor shadow behaviours that arise, learn from them, and convert to the golden. All roles depict and use mostly golden behaviours. The need for decency is paramount.

Gold—continuous balance between golden and shadow behaviours for a leader or the organisation. The balance shifts and changes occasionally, but the golden is present at least 75% of the time. Shadow behaviours exist but are not significant enough to negate the impact of the golden. The shadow is being addressed slowly but surely. Roles depict and use golden behaviours. People try to be decent most times.

Silver—balance between golden and shadow, but the golden is variable and not present over 50% of the time. Daily events and circumstances influence the presence and use of golden or shadow behaviours. There are some efforts to promote the golden, but very few to deal with the shadow side. Roles focus on the use of shadow behaviours with a few golden behaviours. Decency matters only to some.

Bronze—preponderance of shadow behaviours. These are present 75% of the time or more, sometimes masquerading as golden behaviours. Acceptance and normalisation of shadow behaviours occur. There are token attempts to promote golden behaviours, but people recognise that these are not to be taken seriously. Instead, negative behaviours are tacitly and overtly rewarded. Roles encourage the use of shadow behaviours. There are very few attempts to be decent.

The table in the Appendix provides some explanations.

We are ……………………….. because………………………….
……………………………………………………………………………
……………………………………………………………………………
……………………………………………………………………………
……………………………………………………………………………
……………………………………………………………………………
……………………………………………………………………………
……………………………………………………………………………
……………………………………………………………………………
……………………………………………………………………………
……………………………………………………………………………

SHARING AND LEARNING

Once you have gathered all the data, take time to analyse and cross-check your findings. You could present them to a large group of stakeholders who can then look at the results, validate them, and use them to think about the future.

It could help to ask members of the group to look at the findings from both the golden and the shadow perspective.

You could also produce a report using the key areas, and that is your prerogative. It is your choice.

An alternative would be to create a podcast with everyone involved. People could then listen to the podcast in a room with art materials, including paper, and record their reactions and responses to what they are learning. You could collect what they have written or drawn into a huge collage and look at it and reflect. When you feel ready, discuss, and summarise the major learning points.

Make sure that you ask: Now that I/we have looked at the known, what is the unknown that I/we need to uncover and address? What have we not noticed?

Please remember to consider the golden and the shadow and the counterpoints.

> *So, that was a very difficult three months, planning and carrying out the assessment. Finally, we know who supports us, and who wants to be positive, decent and address the negative. We must find a way of helping the toxic individuals change or else they need to leave. Thank goodness we used a collaborative approach.*

⚡⚡

> *We were being productive even though we had a high turnover rate. I really don't know why the board insisted on us doing the exercise. I hope they like the results. We, the executive team, do not. Apparently, it is our fault. Well, let the board try to make changes based on the findings. Good luck to them.*

THE PATH
OF CHANGE
(INDIVIDUAL AND
ORGANISATIONAL)

The path of change

Although the diagram above is linear, change is not. There are many factors that are involved. The work of Dick Beckhard, William Bridges, Elizabeth Kubler Ross, James Prochaska, and

Carlo Di Clemente inspired the diagram. It describes the key elements of change that most individuals and groups go through and experience as they change.

When planning to lead change in an organisation, it is important to understand how individuals and groups are likely to respond. Use the diagram to map where people are in relation to readiness, and what their likely path is going to be. The best option is to show the diagram and ask them. Often, people appreciate a figure like the one above, as it presents a clear roadmap to the future.

Some may go through the path as depicted above, while others will miss one or two elements. Each individual and group is different.

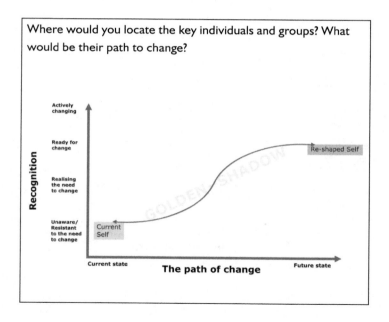

INTERVENTIONS

Here, we offer a wide range of interventions for you to consider. Remember to think of how the people in the organisation are now and what is their scope for change. Try to choose a wider scope than usual. Think about how they can adapt their current ways slowly so that they can transform. It is better to start with adapting rather than trying to force people into new habits. Always involve leaders, managers, and staff when designing and creating the new. They are more likely to choose what will work and be more willing to take part in a change that they have co-designed.

We use the concept of **overall healthiness** to describe incorporating living with the shadow side. The elements are interrelated and co-dependent.

The key aspects of **overall healthiness** are:

> Organisational sense of Self and coordination—compassion, respect, decency, well-being, mental health, physical health, emotions,

cognitions, physical (body), relationships, hope, courage, risk-taking, and motivation

Organisational history

Presence and use of golden and shadow behaviours

Values, ethics, and purpose

Interacting with the wider world and community—material resources and the environment, where a person lives and works

Diversity, equity, and inclusion

Administrative issues

Formal and informal leadership and relationships (including internal culture)

One element, without others, is not enough to become a healthier organisation. However, this is a massive agenda. Please remember to choose what is vital and doable, and that will challenge and stretch the organisation. Please also make your interventions practical and behavioural. Easy for us to say, we know.

Pause for a few moments to honour history and its role in the organisation's present and future. What needs to be brought forward, and what needs to be left behind?

You can adapt all the recommendations below.

A. ORGANISATIONAL SENSE OF SELF AND COORDINATION

Compassion, respect, and decency

It is important for everyone to have compassion for themselves and each other. Without true respect and decency, compassion can lead to selfishness. You will be compassionate with anyone you interact with if you align your regard for them with compassion. This means that you shift from giving so you feel better, to sharing and supporting with dignity.

It is vital to incorporate regular practices, individually and collectively. How can workdays and meetings start with a reminder of compassion, respect, and decency? You can do this by adopting some practices outlined below, but they must occur regularly to have an effect. Think about how individuals or a group could use them.

Here are some interventions.

Create a time during the day to think about being compassionate. Write about those moments when you have shown compassion, respect, and decency. How did others feel? Think about when others showed you compassion, respect, and decency. How did you feel?

Choose a picture or memory that depicts compassion (or respect or decency) for you. Sit quietly and slow down your breathing. As it slows down, clear your mind, and dismiss any stray thoughts that appear. Now, in silence, focus on the picture or memory for five minutes. Then think about how this practice shifted your thoughts, feelings, and body. How can you sustain this during the day?

Deliberate about a sentence that helps you think of being compassionate. Here is one:

> *'We should, each of us, in all our choices, aim to produce the greatest happiness we can and especially the least misery.'*

> Richard Layard

Now write an essay about what this means to you in your life. Save the essay and reread it weekly to remind yourself.

Openness to the future: What can you do to ensure that you remain compassionate and decent with respect, flexible, and open to the future? Perhaps you could allocate some time each day to pause, clear your mind, time, and heart, and just listen. What will you do to always honour this time?

Compassion, respect, and decency in teams are best gained by activating the key elements of emotional intelligence.

Increasing interpersonal understanding involves making efforts to learn what work preferences team members have and then incorporating them. How can you give people more control over their jobs?

Meaningful accountability, collective ownership, and responsibility also need to be encouraged so that people feel they are part of a greater mission.

Team identity and group evaluation, with increasing awareness, are other factors to be encouraged. How does the team function? How can they learn from mistakes without blame? What can they do to praise each other more?

Team Self and group evaluation, with increasing awareness, are other factors to be encouraged. How did we work? Learn from our mistakes without blame? How can we praise each other more?

It is now time to choose your actions and behaviours to bring into reality your intention for the Organisational Self, compassion, respect, and decency.

Which behaviours do you want to use to encourage greater compassion and respect with decency? For example, you could ask people to set aside 10 minutes at the start of the day to reflect on compassion and respect and how they will show it in their work, or you could make time to praise yourself and colleagues.

1.

2.

3.

4.

What cues and triggers do you need to embed the behaviours? For example, you could set an alarm reminding you to be contemplative or ask someone to check in with you about your progress. Remember, it takes 30 days for a new habit to embed itself in people's behaviour, so you may need to be patient.

Building collective accountability for decency

For collective accountability we need a good and trusted internal justice system. Ask people to look at the current internal justice system (ombudspeople, reporting and investigation systems, and psychosocial support), and identify what works, and what needs to change or be removed. And what processes can be put into place to allow people to praise and talk more about observed positive behaviours? What meetings and opportunities could there be for reporting and discussing negativity, so that people can collectively address it? You could have an anonymous reporting system as a start, which could later be supplemented by having a regular forum for talking about solving negativity in the organisational culture.

Well-being, mental health, and physical health

Like compassion, well-being, mental health, and physical health have become very popular interventions in most sectors, especially during the COVID pandemic. Most well-being programmes have a range of components: stress management, self-care, opportunities to learn about mindfulness, yoga, regular health checks, exercise, etc.

What, in the organisation, helps people maintain their well-being, physical health, and mental health? What else is needed?

> Ask people to create a self-care plan and use it. Key areas for personal well-being and self-care include physical and mental health, relationships, financial and material resources, work, and colleagues. What is working in each area and what needs to change? A manager's role should only be to ask if a plan exists. Anything more may require the staff member to divulge confidential information.

If there has been toxicity, then people may need extra support and help to regain their well-being. This includes those who have been perpetrators. An independent mental health professional or an internal expert who has the authority to maintain confidentiality should provide this support.

Team well-being depends on many factors. The diagram below outlines the key factors that impact team well-being. Why not use it with your team to determine what is working in terms of well-being, and what they can change? What just needs to be accepted?

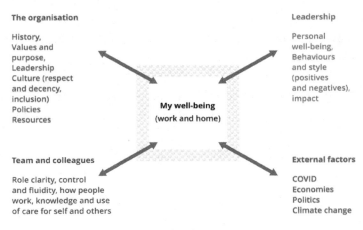

The organisation

History,
Values and
purpose,
Leadership
Culture (respect
and decency,
inclusion)
Policies
Resources

Leadership

Personal
well-being,
Behaviours
and style
(positives
and negatives),
impact

**My well-being
(work and home)**

Team and colleagues

Role clarity, control
and fluidity, how people
work, knowledge and use
of care for self and others

External factors

COVID
Economies
Politics
Climate change

Emotions, cognitions, physical (body), and relationships

People's levels of well-being, mental health, and physical health affect these. So, it is vital that the organisation encourages people to look after themselves as well as supporting people when they become ill, take time off and then return to work.

Hope, courage, risk-taking, and motivation

Each organisation will have its own approach to these factors; leaders (formal and informal) set the tone. For constructive risk-taking, we need a positive amount of courage alongside realistic amounts of hope and motivation. What can we do to help leaders and others feel strong enough to have hope, feel motivated, and take good risks?

B. ORGANISATIONAL HISTORY

This always impacts everyday life. It is worth exploring this so that the positive aspects can be honoured and the negative addressed. Who are the holders of the history and how can they be engaged to build the positive? How can they be encouraged to let go of the negative aspects and attitudes?

C. PRESENCE AND USE OF GOLDEN AND SHADOW BEHAVIOURS

Our shadow side is part of us and very unlikely to disappear. We must learn how to decrease its effect and to live more in balance between the golden and the shadow side. Regular pause and reflection can do this. Here are some exercises to try, either as an individual or group.

Start practices where you praise staff—both colleagues and leaders—for the positive and let them know they can speak openly about any negatives they may observe or experience. They need to feel that they can do this without retribution.

Use these practices individually or as a group. Please adapt them as needed.

Find a quiet and comfortable place (perhaps with a trusted person).

Write or draw your shadow side. Sit with your output and let your emotions arise. Wait until they have dissipated, then explore the purpose and function of these shadow actions and behaviours. Which parts of your golden side can help to counterbalance them? Then think about which shadow behaviours you could replace with a positive aspect, and which you could release.

On a second piece of paper, write or draw the replacement behaviours and emotions. Stop and let yourself feel. Then, when you are ready, say goodbye and destroy the first piece of paper or art. Keep the remaining paper or art for another time.

This is an exercise you can repeat as often as you want.

Imagine talking to your shadow aspects and ask which need to stay or go. How can the golden help with the shadow side? What has happened to the Self? Make a note of your reflections.

You could, on a daily or weekly basis, make some time to reflect on the extent to which you have lived and worked from your golden side and/or shadow side. What did you learn, and how will you cope from now on?

You could use the diagram below to reflect on your week. In which quadrant did you live and work? What have you learned, and what needs to be improved or let go of?

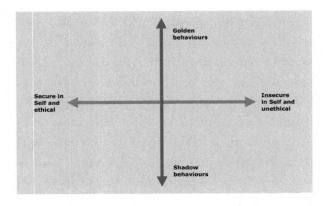

〰〰

If you are someone who has dwelled on the shadow side and are ready to shift to using more golden aspects of yourself, then please start with celebrating the golden.

What is wonderful about you and your sense of Self?

Then note down your shadow parts and think about what you need to let go to move to the golden side. Who and what will help you? What is the path you want to take?

Sometimes, large changes are too much. You could start with small steps, such as not ignoring people (if that is one of your behaviours) and making sure you greet colleagues. Some people may not believe the change at first, but if you persist, they are likely to adjust their perspective of you.

〰〰

Imagine a long line in a room with *Golden* at one end and *Shadow* at the other. Stand in the shadow part and look ahead to the golden side. Imagine that you are being accompanied by your best friend, *Decency.* Start walking towards the golden part and imagine how you feel as you are moving towards it. Once you have arrived at the golden part, stop, and think about what/who else could have helped you on your journey. What would your best friend, *Decency*, say? What have you learned about yourself? This could become a weekly practice.

〰〰

Based on her research with healing indigenous communities, Dr. Sousan Abadian has created the Awareness, Responsibility, Imagination, Action (ARIA) framework, which can explore the shadow side. She intended it for healing individual and community trauma. The first step is to notice oneself and the erroneous assumptions, beliefs, and narratives.

Second, she advises the person or group to consider their assumptions, beliefs, and narratives, and rewrite or replace them so that they are more positive and aspirational.

Third, it is time to become open to inspiration and the possibility of what the person or community wants to be and focus on that instead of the current perspectives. She guides people to use the aspirations to design next steps and act as though the desired future is here.

〰〰

Think about your life and how much balance there is between the golden and shadow sides. How would you describe this? How constant is the balance? What is the function and purpose of the balance for you? What could you do to ensure a healthier and more constant balance?

If you have identified individuals who operate from the shadow side and are toxic, then it is important to think about what you can do. Some may be amenable to changing and others may not. You can discuss their past behaviours with them and let them know what you expect in the future. For a very few, the only option may be to facilitate their departure from the organisation.

D. VALUES, ETHICS, AND PURPOSE

Most employees hope to fulfill their personal purpose and, at least, have it match that of the organisation. The reality is often very different. We must acknowledge and discuss this, so that there is honesty about the compromise that is present.

E. INTERACTING WITH THE WIDER WORLD AND COMMUNITY

Material resources and the environment

These influence employees and are vital. Identify what you should provide to ensure that staff have suitable work environments and include efforts to support the need for sustainability. It is important to factor in the impact of external culture and events such as COVID.

Where people live and work

Be honest about what is possible in terms of resources for work. People appreciate the truth.

Some of us struggle with the concept of hybrid working because we have massive physical assets that we can't get rid of, or we need to be in control by being able to see people. It is better to think about the crucial tasks and roles for achieving the organisation's purpose. What resources are needed? Then think about where people need to be physically. How can you have a multi-faceted hybrid work model that allows as much flexibility as possible?

F. DIVERSITY, EQUITY, AND INCLUSION

People need genuine diversity, equity, and inclusion across the organisation, so that no one feels excluded because of their individual characteristics or background. What do you need to ensure better inclusion within the organisation? Would diverse staff agree with you?

Remember that toxicity often impedes inclusion. How can you ensure that there are minimal amounts of toxicity and that when it arises, you tackle it while promoting the positive? Do the behaviours of some people in the organisation need to be addressed? What policies and structures need to change? How can you encourage everyone to promote collective accountability for positive behaviours, and name and tackle the negative ones when they arise?

G. ADMINISTRATIVE ISSUES

There may well be some administrative issues that need to be addressed, e.g., reviewing current HR policies to ensure that they promote golden and not shadow behaviours. Note what needs updating and work out a plan for change.

Another vital issue is having a trusted internal justice system, including a complaints procedure and an ombudsperson. You could think about introducing one or seeing what you need to make the existing system more effective and trusted.

H. FORMAL AND INFORMAL LEADERSHIP AND RELATIONSHIPS (INCLUDING INTERNAL CULTURE)

Someone once said that the smallest unit of an organisation is two people talking. Consider how you can promote positive and supportive relationships and well-being in the various teams. How can you acknowledge and thank the formal and informal leaders and supporters?

If there are cliques, how can you discourage them once you have identified them? Think about why they exist—insecurity, a desire for power, feeling disgruntled. Talk to the staff and ask them to think about how they can support each other more positively.

Organisations use a wide range of interventions, from coaching to leadership programmes to enhance leadership skills. If you select some of them, then they must address the positive with the negative and enable people to practice what they have learned.

PLANS FOR CHANGE

Here are some steps to take to devise a plan for change. Remember to build this with all concerned.

Looking at the key areas for overall healthiness in the table below—which interventions will you select? Where do you want to be: platinum, gold, silver, or bronze? Please have a look at the Appendix for ideas as well.

What will be the future sense of Organisational Self? What type of organisation do you want to be? What is your promise, either to the organisation or the wider world?

Therefore, what will be the key elements of your plan, and who will help? Here is a template.

Area	Description	Timeframe/Helpers
Sense of Organisational Self and coordination		

Compassion, respect, and decency		
Building collective accountability		
Well-being, mental health, and physical health		
Emotions, cognitions, physical (body), and relationships		
Hope, courage, risk-taking, and motivation		
Organisational history		
Presence and use of golden and shadow behaviours		
Values, ethics, and purpose		
Interacting with the wider world and community		

Material re-sources and the environment		
Where people live and work		
Diversity, equity, and inclusion		
Administrative issues		
Formal and informal leadership and relationships (including internal culture)		
Anything else		

Well, the board forced us to develop a change plan for collective accountability. We must admit we did not refer to it or implement it for the first three months. Then we were asked to meet with staff who had suffered because of negative behaviours. Oh, what a shock. There is more than productivity that should matter. We have now committed to the plan, and we are seeing it through. We will each have to stop and change. What did we do to contribute to the awfulness?

The plan for collective accountability is working. At first, no one was willing to talk about what was positive, and what was negative and needed to be reported. I, as Chief Executive, started the process by having these discussions with the executive team. This then encouraged the leaders and managers to have more open discussions in their departments.

A REALITY CHECK

This is an opportunity to make sure that the plans you have made are realistic and ready. What changes do you need to make?

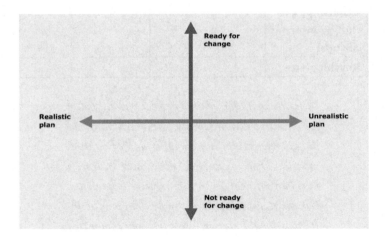

Thank you, and we wish you the very best on your journey.
www.healthyleadership.world
Instagram: healthyleadership.world

REFERENCES

These are available on our website:
www.healthyleadership.world.

APPENDIX

THE HEALTHY ORGANISATION INDEX

Overall health level	Platinum	Gold	Silver	Bronze
Area/elements				
Organisational sense of Self and roles	Very positive, compassionate, realistic, and respectful. Decency is very present. Connected harmoniously with other elements.	Positive, compassionate, realistic, and respectful. Decency is present. Connected harmoniously sometimes with other elements.	Spasmodically positive, compassionate, realistic, and respectful. Little evidence of decency Occasionally in synchrony with other elements or negative.	Negative and disrespectful. No decent behavours used. Rarely connected to other elements or negative.

Building collective accountability	Leadership, by example, fully encourages collective accountability and has appropriate internal justice systems in place.	Leadership encourages collective accountability most of the time.	Leadership promotes our own version of collective accountability. We praise the positive behaviours of a few. We do not address the negative much.	There is a complete lack of collective accountability. Leadership's version of accountability focuses on what we deem important.
Well-being, mental health, and physical health	The well-being, mental health, and physical health of all staff is paramount.	The well-being, mental health, and physical health of most staff is important.	The well-being, mental health, and physical health of some staff is important.	The well-being, mental health and physical health of staff is not important, except for the chosen few.
Cognitions, emotions, physical (body), culture, work practices, and relationships (including leadership)	The focus of both the culture and relationships is always on healthiness, including diversity, equity, and inclusion. We treat all staff with utmost respect. We encourage positive relationships all the time.	The focus of both the culture and relationships is on healthiness, including diversity, equity, and inclusion. We treat most staff with a lot of respect. We encourage positive relationships most of the time.	The focus of both the culture and relationships is sometimes on healthiness, including diversity, equity, and inclusion. We treat some staff with respect. We allow cliques and in-groups that benefit the few.	The focus of both the culture and relationships is rarely on healthiness, including diversity, equity, and inclusion. We respect only a few staff. We encourage punitive cliques and in-groups.

	Thinking, decision-making, and work practices are helpful and effective. We quickly deal with any shadow behaviours that arise.	Thinking, decision-making, and work practices are sometimes helpful and effective. We deal with most shadow behaviours that arise.	Thinking, decision-making, and work practices are rarely helpful and effective. We deal with some shadow behaviours that arise.	Thinking, decision-making, and work practices are not helpful or effective. We allow and encourage shadow behaviours.
Hope, courage, risk-taking, and motivation.	Leadership shows all these characteristics, and this encourages others.	Leadership shows some of these characteristics most of the time, which then encourages others.	Leadership shows few of these characteristics.	Leadership shows none of these characteristics except to meet their own needs.
Organisational history	We honour and learn from history; we celebrate anniversaries.	We acknowledge and sometimes learn from history.	We ignore history.	We totally deny the importance of history unless it reinforces our current toxic zeitgeist.
Presence and use of golden and shadow behaviours	Golden>Shadow 95% Nearly all understand and use golden behaviours and identify and address shadow behaviours.	Golden>Shadow 75% Most understand and use golden behaviours. We address and sometimes change if there are shadow behaviours.	Golden=Shadow 50% Very few understand and use golden behaviours, and many do not address the use of shadow behaviours.	Golden<Shadow 25% Shadow behaviours are the norm, golden behaviours are rare and unrewarded.

Values, ethics, and purpose	These are core, understood, and lived by all.	These are central, understood, and used.	People know them, but only use them sometimes.	We ignore these unless it is to others' advantage.
Interacting with the wider world and community	There is synergy with the wider world, and sustainability for all is a prime goal.	There is some synergy and connectedness with the wider world and community.	We note the wider world and community's presence, but do not factor it in significantly.	We ignore the needs of the wider world or use them to the advantage of the organisation.
Where people work	Excellent care and thought have gone into this, and staff feel very comfortable. We know of and resource all adjustments for diverse needs.	A lot of care and thought have gone into this, and staff feel comfortable. We know of and resource most adjustments for diverse needs.	Some care and thought have gone into this, and staff sometimes feel comfortable. We know of and resource some adjustments for diverse needs.	Very limited care and thought have gone into this, and staff feel uncomfortable. We know of and resource a few adjustments for diverse needs.
Diversity, equity, and inclusion	Inclusion is at the centre of the organization. Respect for all is evident.	There are significant attempts to include as many people as possible with differences.	There are some surface attempts to be inclusive, e.g., posters but there is little action.	There is very little done to be inclusive. The favoured few are looked after. Other's needs are ignored or ridiculed.

Administrative matters: legislation, policies, procedures, and organisational structures	All administrative elements are supportive of the aims of a healthy organisation. Where needed, we fully implement them.	Most administrative elements are supportive of the aims of a healthy organisation. Where needed, we implement most of them.	Some administrative elements are supportive of the aims of a healthy organisation. Where needed, we sometimes implement them.	Very few administrative elements are supportive of the aims of a healthy organisation. Even if needed, we rarely implement them.
Formal and informal leaderships	All formal and informal leaders work in tandem and democratically. Open consultation and communication exist. All staff are given opportunities to learn and develop and then implement what they have learned at work.	Formal and informal leaders collaborate most of the time through consultation and communication. Some learning opportunities are available to most staff.	Formal and informal leaders sometimes work together with some consultation and communication. Only the favoured few benefit from learning. Implementing what they have learned is not important.	Very limited collaboration and cooperation. Formal and informal leaders often work against each other. There is no real attempt to encourage staff to learn and develop.
Anything else?				

Printed in Great Britain
by Amazon